Title

FEELING OF SIX FRIENDS

Preface

"They're five minutes late," I declared to the table, looking at the two void seats in the middle.

My companions and I, alongside thirty different visitors, were sat in an enormous, babble filled meal lobby in Seattle for my dearest companion, Mara's commitment party. We were, notwithstanding, missing Mara and her life partner, Will.

"Perhaps she's actually preparing," mine and Mara's dearest companion Allison, presented as a reason to attempt to assuage me.

Wishing that was valid however realizing it wasn't, I said, "I prepared her myself. They ought to be here. I'm simply going to call Mara, and-"

My beau, Dru, unexpectedly cut me off, getting my telephone. "No, you're not. I'm certain they'll be here soon, Bri. Presently, partake in the party.

"OK, give me my telephone back," I demanded going after it, however he essentially threw it to my twin sibling, Carter.

"Assuming we give this back to you," Carter began, "you set it aside and let Mara and Will show up at whatever point they need to.

"Fine," I concurred, taking my telephone back. " I won't call until they're fifteen minutes late. By then, it's simply unsatisfactory. I could never permit this from any of my different customers."

Carter murmured. "They're an extraordinary different customers, Sabrina. Mara's your closest companion."

Dru participated. "Also you're the same amount of a visitor as you are the wedding organizer. You've been working really hard for quite a long time. You have the right to unwind and live it up.

I let out a cut snicker. "There's no an ideal opportunity to unwind. They allowed me five months to assemble Mara's fantasy wedding. I assisted Mara with arranging her fantasy wedding when we were ten, and it hasn't changed a little. Do you know what sort of weddings ten-year-olds cook up? Large ones, ones that require over five months to assemble!"

Allison, Dru, and Carter checked out me attentively, and Dru painstakingly ventured into my tote and took out two caffeinated drinks.

"I think you've had enough of these," he said, giving them to Carter who put them on a passing servers plate.

"I want those," I cried, watching the server leave with my sole wellspring of energy.

"No, you really want rest," Dru amended.

"I rest."

"Definitely, for around three hours consistently."

"It's sufficient."

"Obviously not. This is the most worried I've at any point seen you over a wedding."

Allison jeered and feigned exacerbation. "I'm not sure what the serious deal is. It'll be in every way over in a month and a half in any case, and afterward we would all be able to approach the remainder of our lives not contemplating or recollect this damn wedding."

She took an enormous swallow of the champagne before her, and I looked on with concern, something about the remark not agreeing with me. It evidently didn't agree with Dru either, at the same time, in contrast to me, he had no issue let Allison know what he thought about her, which wasn't especially may I add.

"What the heck is your concern, Allison? You've had a stick up your butt since the time Will proposed. You two have been over for five years at this point. Deal with it."

"I'm over it," she demanded. "How should I not be the point at which I have Carter? I unmistakably profited from the separation."

"You are so brimming with bullsh-"

"Both of you, shut up," Carter requested. "They're coming."

A fast look toward the entry uncovered that he was correct, and I immediately turned my consideration back to Allison and Dru. "Squash this now, and put blesses your countenances. Assuming you mess this up, I'll make your lives hopeless. Do you get it?"

They gestured, saving each other a last glare prior to sticking grins onto their appearances as Mara and Will went into the room. Arms connected, they got out and about by any stretch of the imagination of different tables prior to advancing toward the unfilled seats hanging tight for them at our table.

"You're late," I murmured to my closest companion as she subsided into her seat to one side.

"Quiet down, Sabrina. We were simply stranded in rush hour gridlock," she informed me grinning to herself.

"Better believe it, I'm certain," I murmured, squinting my eyes at her, knowing precisely what she implied by "trapped in rush hour gridlock."

I took out my telephone and settled on a fast decision to the top of the catering staff. When I hung up, servers rose up out of an entryway on the right half of the room and started to serve the visitors. I discovered Mara checking out the clamoring room with stunningness and energy.

"I did a very steady employment didn't I?" I murmured energetically, bumping her shoulder.

She gave a little snicker, shaking her head. "I can't really accept that this is really occurring."

"Indeed, accept this is on the grounds that, in a month and a half, no doubt about it."

"Also shouldn't something be said about you?" She asked suddenly, surprising me.

"What?"

"At the point when will you get hitched," she explained, making me feign exacerbation.

"At the point when it's the ideal opportunity. It probably won't make any difference at the present time. This is your chance to hit one out of the ballpark.

She lifted her hands in mock acquiescence. "All I'm saying is that it's been eight years, and-

"Mara, stop. You generally do this."

"Continuously do what?" She asked, faking blamelessness.

"Divert the consideration at whatever point it's on you. Indeed, prepare to have your mind blown. All of this is for you. The consideration is all on you, and it's basically impossible to keep away from it."

She peered down at her plate, realizing I'd got her. Whenever everybody was served and the servers had gotten out, I stood, catching everybody's eye by gently tapping my fork on my champagne woodwind.

"I might want to give an impromptu speech to my dearest companion, Mara. We've been dreaming about this since we were ten, and I am happy to the point that you at long last get to have it. You have a stunning man who couldn't be more ideal for you," I accentuated, shooting an admonition view at Allison as she polished off her second glass of champagne and motioned to the server to bring another. "I am so glad for you. No one has the right to have their glad closure more than you do. I love you and congrats."

Mara remained to embrace me as the visitors acclaimed and we retook our seats. Realizing it was his move, Dru remained to give his discourse.

"Alright, I'm clearly not going to top that, so I'll keep it short. Will, it took you a couple of attempts, yet you at long last hit the nail on the head." I didn't miss his tricky glance at Allison who was giving no consideration as she waved to the server for another glass. "Mara's a guardian, so clutch her, man. Well done."

Everybody commended once more, and Will remained to brother embrace Dru prior to sitting down.

"Might any other individual want to give a toast for the benefit of this exquisite couple?" I declared, glancing around.

Likely stirring up a lot of worry for everybody at the table, Allison lifted her hand. "I would."

Carter unpretentiously gave her an admonition look, however Allison just feigned exacerbation, polished off her fourth glass and stood in any case.

"To Will and Mara. Who would've imagined that it would keep going this long? That is to say, as indicated by Sabrina's outlines in general and charts, you folks shouldn't work, yet you have challenged the chances. Here's to trusting that you continue to disprove the stars."

The acclaim was delayed to begin and sort of uncomfortable. Mara and Will moved awkwardly in their seats. Dru was glaring a hold in Allison, who carelessly waved to the server for a fifth glass of champagne. My sibling appeared to be abruptly exceptionally inspired by his prepared potato, and I restlessly supported my head in my grasp, previously feeling a headache coming on

.

Chapter 1: Woe And Fear

After seven days I was back home in Tampa, making an honest effort to sooth a still jumpy Mara via telephone, yet it was turning out to be exceptionally obvious that I was facing a losing conflict. It was going on two hours as I imploded on my sofa with the telephone on speaker.

"I don't have the foggiest idea what you need me to tell you, Mar."

"Let me know that what Ali said was off-base and that the stars aren't neutralizing Will and me."

"I can't let you know that," I conceded. "I cautioned you when you two began dating that Gemini and Virgo are contrary."

"All things considered, possibly you weren't right."

I laughed at her suggestion. "I wasn't, however what difference does it make? You don't trust in soothsaying."

"I know, however imagine a scenario in which there is a trace of validity in it."

"Gracious, there's certainly truth in it," I told her as Dru arose out of the kitchen, a mug close by. "A great deal of truth, yet I don't think the stars are what you truly called to converse with me about. What's truly continuing?"

I quietly hung tight for Mara's answer as Dru gave me the mug and sat down, maneuvering me into his lap. I settled against him, giving him a concise, content grin prior to turning my consideration back to my telephone as Mara talked once more.

"I couldn't say whether I feel OK with Allison being a bridesmaid any longer. That is to say, she's probably my closest companion, yet after the party last week... "

I gestured despite the fact that she was unable to see me. "I get that, and-"

She immediately cut me off. "I know, I know. As a Gemini, five is one of my fortunate numbers, so it would be ideal to have five bridesmaids," she said, impersonating my voice.

Dru laughed unobtrusively at Mara's right on target impression, however I, being less entertained, immediately shut him with a glare, and he unexpectedly observed the example of our lounge chair extremely intriguing.

"Indeed, indeed, however that is not what I planned to say. I planned to say that this is your wedding and your decision. I for one don't think you have anything to stress over. Will is an incredible person, and he could never really hurt you," I remedied.

Mara murmured. "I know, yet their set of experiences truly bothers me. I can't resist the urge to feel like she has some mysterious arrangement to demolish my life. Dru, what is your take?"

Dru and I shared a delighted grin before I turned my consideration back to the current matter. "What makes you think Dru is here?"

"Dru is consistently there some place, and now and again he offers preferable guidance over you. What's your agreement, Dru? Do I have anything to stress over?"

"In case you're getting some information about Allison, I'm not going to mislead you and say that she's making an effort not to get Will back. I'm around 95% sure that she is," Dru illuminated her, all hints of delight gone. "In case you're inquiring as to whether there's any possibility that will return to her after she broke his heart, I will say no. Will is infatuated with you. You're really amazing thing that is at any point happened to him. Try not to question that."

I could perceive that Dru's words gave Mara
some alleviation as she inhaled a little murmur,
and I grinned up at my beau, dazzled however
not astonished by his master warning abilities.

"So what's the arrangement, Mara?" I asked. "Am
I removing Allison from the wedding?"

"No. She can remain. Everything will turn out
great," she finished up.

"Express gratitude toward God," I relaxed. "That
would have been a bad dream to adjust. I'll call
you tomorrow," I said, prepared to get off the
telephone.

"Okay, much appreciated, both of you."

"Don't sweat it," I answered while Dru said,
"Whenever."

I immediately hung up the telephone and sat it on
the end table, taking a taste of my tea, then, at
that point, going to check out Dru.

"Good gracious," he began. "I realize that look. What's going on?"

"I don't have the foggiest idea," I conceded. "I simply have a genuinely terrible inclination about this entire thing. Do you believe that Allison will begin something?"

Dru murmured profoundly. "Typically, I'd say no. She's not so insane, but rather love causes individuals to do insane things."

I felt my eyes enlarge at the idea. "You believe she's as yet infatuated with him?"

He just gestured. "I do."

Then, at that point, one more idea hit me. "My sibling "

"Isn't negligent. Carter knows how she is. He simply will do nothing about it."

I shook my head, putting it in my grasp like I generally do when I get restless. Dru put a hand

on my back encouragingly, focusing on it little
circles that right away quieted me down.

"Quiet down, Bri. You're becoming upset over a
lot of things that are out of your control."

I moaned, reclining against the sofa. "I don't think
I'll have the option to quiet down until this
wedding is finished."

Chapter 2: Analogy

I love Wednesdays. I get off of work early, and I get to return home and eat with Allison. It was consistently the most laid back and pleasant piece of my week, however something let me know that this Wednesday would not have been as old as strolled into mine and Allison's Boston condo and thought that she is perched on the arm of the love seat hanging tight for me eagerly.

"What is it?" I asked carefully, the examine her eyes saying she needed to discuss something genuine.

"I simply need to talk," she answered. "Come sit with me."

I put my satchel somewhere near the entryway, and joined my better half, hanging tight for her to begin discussing what she needed to discuss.

"What's happening?" I asked when she a tad.

"For what reason haven't you proposed to me yet, Carter?"

I was so shocked that I just squinted at her idiotically, attempting to enroll the inquiry that had appeared unexpectedly.

"I... uh... I simply don't believe we're prepared for that yet, Ali," I clarified, still somewhat shaken at the inquiry.

"No difference either way. Don't you cherish me?"

"Obviously, I love you, Allison, yet that doesn't imply that we ought to simply proceed to get hitched. That is to say, check out Sabrina and Dru. They've been together for quite some time and they're in no surge."

Allison feigned exacerbation at the notice of my sister. "Definitely, yet it's Sabrina we're discussing. Everything must be impeccably arranged out for her, and the sort of flawlessness she searches for sets aside time. We're not them, Carter. We're not dealing with some nonexistent clock constrained by the stars. We're working continuously. We've been together similarly insofar as Will and Mara, and we haven't talked about marriage.

I moaned defeatedly, resting my head in my grasp as I at last enlisted what was going on with this. Since the time we got together, she's been fixated on one-increasing Will and Mara, and I'm not completely certain why. What I made certain of, in any case, is that this whole discussion was a piece of her fixation, and I wasn't going to have it.

"I see," I murmured, thinking back up at her.

"You see what?"

"I see the reason why we aren't prepared to get hitched. This isn't about you and me by any stretch of the imagination. This is about your fanatical need to consistently outshine Mara since you're desirous of her and Will.

"What? No, it's not," she said unconvincingly. "Carter, I-"

"For what reason are you even with me, Allison?" I inquired. "Is this is on the grounds that you would not allow Will to win? You just needed to show that you were in an ideal situation without him, so you proceeded to get yourself a fruitful legal counselor. Is that it?"

"What, Carter? Obviously not!"

"I'm struggling trusting you, Allison," I conceded.

"Carter, you realize that is not it. I love you."

"You love me?" I watched her gesture her head promptly, however I actually couldn't force myself to trust her. "Look me in my eyes and let me know that you're not ledge in adoration with Will."

"I'm not as yet infatuated with Will. I love you, and just you."

Despite the fact that she looked at me straightforwardly without flinching and talked gradually and plainly, making a point to articulate each and every word, it felt thought up, and I stayed unconvinced, so I gestured and stood. Getting my portfolio, I strolled toward my work space.

"Carter, where are you going?" She asked, getting up to follow me.

"I have some work to finish," I addressed without further ado.

"Be that as it may, we haven't eaten at this point. Wednesdays are the main time you get off right on time."

"I'm not ravenous," I lied, turning my back to her and vanishing a few doors down.

"Carter! Hell. Carter, please," she asked, however I was unable to think that it is in myself to react or return.

Chapter 3: Anxiety

"Do you figure I could convince Mara to have the wedding a day after the fact?" I asked Dru, as I remained before my crystal gazing and arranging sheets in our work space with a dry eradicate marker in one hand and a pushpin in the other.

"Likely not," he answered, coming into the workplace and following my look to my star graphs. I could perceive that he comprehended that whatever I was seeing wasn't agreeing with me. "Presently, kindly put the marker and yarn down and how about we pick a film."

I shook my head, glaring passionately at the diagrams. "I can't until I sort out some solution for this looming wreck.

"Sabrina, there's no way around the date. Mara won't ever transform it dependent on something that she doesn't have faith in," he contemplated.

"Alright, perhaps I read the stars wrong," I offered, realizing he was correct and searching for another exit from the shitstorm that was coming.

"Right, and what are the possibilities that you wrecked a star outline?" He asked snidely, puncturing my rationale.

"Thin," I mumbled, "yet at the same certainly feasible. Simply give me like 60 minutes, and afterward I'm all yours, OK?"

I realized I was in a difficult situation when Dru said nothing, yet I wasn't anticipating that he should toss me behind him and convey me into the family room like a cave dweller.

"What's going on with you? Put me down," I shrieked. I got what I requested as Dru indiscreetly dropped me on the sofa prior to sitting down close to me don't like anything had occurred. "What the heck, Dru?"

"You wouldn't put the work down," was his straightforward answer.

"I just required 60 minutes."

"Also last I checked, we shouldn't be dealing with Friday evenings, so I don't believe I'm the one off base here," he snapped, surprising me.

I didn't say anything. I realized he was correct. I realized I was off base. I realized that this wedding was making me insane. Being me, nonetheless, I wasn't willing to concede that without holding back, so I absolutely got up and strolled back toward our office. Dru jeered disbelievingly prior to getting up to stop me. He immediately positioned himself before me to keep me from leaving the room.

"Move, Dru," I requested, keeping away from eye to eye connection.

"Sabrin-"

"Move!"

"No!" He shouted right back. "Sabrina, we set to the side Friday evenings on purpose. This is supportive of you so you can de-stress. You get so ended up over all of this, and for reasons unknown, this particular wedding is negatively affecting you that I've never seen. I have never seen you really hopeless while going about your business up to this point. It's not beneficial. All I'm requesting is one night out of the week for you to put all of this down and loosen up. Is that to an extreme?"

"No... " I murmured, peering down at the floor.

"Much thanks to you. Presently, come on. I'll allow you to pick the film which I'm certain I'll lament later."

"My desire for motion pictures isn't so awful," I said protectively.

"Eh... It's awful."

I snickered delicately as I reviewed the spread of tidbits that Dru had set up on the end table. "Is that guac?"

"Mm-hm."

"For what reason didn't you simply lead with that? It would've saved you such a difficult situation."

Dru checked out me regrettably as he sat down close to me on the love seat. "You are the most goading lady I've at any point met."

"Aw, I love you as well," I said, putting a kiss on his cheek.

Chapter 4:

"What might be said about this one?" I asked, sleepily.

It was seven days after my discussion with Sabrina and Dru, and Will and I were perched on the love seat in our Houston condo, looking through lodging destinations on our individual workstations searching for another house.

I showed him the house on my PC, in a split second knowing from the expression all over that he was not a fan.

"Excessively little," he said. "I like this one."

He showed me his PC, and I dismissed the sheer size of the house, and that was before I checked out the cost. "Is it accurate to say that you are insane? We can't bear the cost of that!"

Will looked befuddled, turning the PC back around to check out it himself. A look of understanding crossed his face, and he laughed delicately, clicking something prior to turning the PC back around.

"Apologies, love. Wrong house. Shouldn't something be said about this one?"

The house looked pleasant, and I was much more intrigued as I looked through the entirety of the conveniences and data. Then, at that point, I saw the cost, and I knew. We had tracked down our home.

"Will, this is awesome. It's somewhere between the rec center and the studio. It's a great size for a family. Furthermore the value, the cost is the most amazing aspect, all things considered,

"Along these lines, we would like to go look at this one tomorrow?" He inquired.

"Obviously we do. For what reason is that even an inquiry?"

Will grinned at my energy and gestured. "Okay, I'll set it up."

He began to type on his telephone, and I watched him, falling profound into thought. I realized that the Allison circumstance at the commitment party was certifiably not no joking matter, however I actually needed to know his opinion on it.

"Will?"

"Hm?"

"Has Allison been acting... off around you of late?"

He gazed toward me confusedly. "Off how?"

I shrugged, peering down at my hands. "She's been somewhat antagonistic since the time the commitment party. You haven't took note?"

"No."

"Her discourse at the party didn't appear to be not quite right to you?" I asked.

"She was inebriated, Mar," he safeguarded, thinking down at his telephone.

"I know, however why? The party had recently begun. What made her beverage to such an extent?"

Will murmured, putting his telephone down on the end table, and going to completely confront me. "You're looking excessively far into this."

"Am I?" I tested.

"Indeed," he answered. "What conceivable explanation could Allison have for being antagonistic? She's content with Carter."

I shook my head. I didn't have the foggiest idea why he was so promptly guarding Allison, however I realized that I was finished with this discussion. "Guess what? Disregard I said anything," I excused, remaining strong with my PC and going to the room.

"Deface "

"You have a tux fitting to get to," I interfered, not having any desire to hear whatever excuse planned to emerge from his mouth.

As though on sign, Sabrina and Dru strolled into the loft conveying covers, and I sent a quiet supplication to God, expressing gratitude toward him for giving me a closest companion with such incredible planning.

"Don't you all thump?" Will snapped, plainly irritated at the interruption.

Dru checked out his closest companion, resolute by the terrible mentality. "You gave us a key since you were worn out on getting up to give us access."

Sabrina didn't say anything, investigating at me. I knew she could peruse me inside and out. She could perceive that I really want to talk and that I needed to do it without the folks present.

"Hello, both of you really want to get rolling, so that is no joke," she reported, tending to Dru and Will.

"We actually have two hours before the fitting," Dru called attention to, checking out his sweetheart in disarray.

"Definitely, however you know how Houston traffic gets," she clarified. "You all should go at this point."

"Bri-"

"Out. Presently," she requested.

Actually like Sabrina could understand me, Dru could understand her. He took a gander at her, and understanding occurred to him seconds after the fact.

"You know what, you're correct," Dru said. "We should go, Will."

"What? It is absolutely impossible that a thirty-minute drive will transform into two hours," Will attempted to reason. "It doesn't matter at all to me how insane the traffic is."

"We should go, Will," Dru rehashed, setting a fast kiss on Sabrina's cheek prior to going to the entryway.

"Fine," Will yielded, going to address Sabrina, "in any case, to make sure you know, I don't like being kicked out of my own condo.'

"Definitely, I'm certain you don't," she said, sounding exhausted. "Presently, get out."

She trusted that Dru and will pass on the condo prior to going to me adequately quick to give herself whiplash. "What'd he do?"

Chapter 5:

After a month, we were all back in Seattle. The wedding was the following day, and Allison, Mara, and I were at supper prior to taking off on the town to cause problems that I had gotten ready for us for the evening.

"I could've gone for what seems like forever without realizing that with regards to my sibling, Ali," I said, taking a major swallow of my wine as I attempted to disregard the exceptionally distinctive picture that Allison had placed to me.

"You folks asked," Allison answered protectively.

Mara gestured. "Also now we think twice about it. I'll never take a gander at Carter the same way again."

I flinched once more. "You truly could've saved us the subtleties."

"All things considered, you ought to have said that."

I shook my head. "I didn't think I'd need to."

Mara chuckled a little as she stood. "I will hit the women's room truly speedy before we go. I'll be right back."

"So how are things with Carter, Ali?" I asked nonchalantly, recollecting how Dru said that he imagined that Allison was as yet infatuated with Will notwithstanding being with my sibling.

She moaned, allowing her head to fall onto the table. "Things were great, yet we got into a contention about a month prior, and things haven't been something very similar."

"A contention concerning what?" I asked, interest promptly aroused.

"He hasn't proposed to me indeed, Bri," she cried.

"What's more?"

"We've been together for quite some time, actually like Will and Mara. Will could think that it is in him to propose. For what reason can't Carter?"

"Gracious, I see," I muttered, attempting to keep a beware of my attitude.

"No doubt, you Hart twins," she protested. "I've had it with your 'I sees.' What the fuck would you say you are seeing that I'm not?"

"Ali, you need to quit contrasting him with Will. He's not Will."

"I realize that," she demanded following off insightfully as she took one more taste of the wine before her. "Perhaps that is the issue."

Freezing in my seat, I checked out Allison like she was insane. "For what reason would that be an issue, Allison?"

She inclined across the table to murmur as though any other individual in the café was focusing on us. "You can't let anybody know that I'm saying this."

I gestured, seeing Mara rise up out of the bathroom somewhere off to the side. She took a gander at me confusedly as she moved toward the table, and I unpretentiously shook my head. She gestured and remained where she was, far away from Allison yet sufficiently close to tune in.

"I feel like Will is my perfect partner," Ali conceded. "We had the ideal relationship, and I just needed to proceed to screw everything up. Presently, I can't have a typical relationship with any other person since I naturally contrast him with Will. Your sibling inquired as to whether I was as yet infatuated with Will, and I told him, no, yet I think I was lying. Does that make me a terrible individual?"

Mara and I were frozen in shock at the affirmation. I saw the tears gushing in Mara's eyes, and could experience the resentment developing in myself and realized that we expected to escape the public eye before this scene got noticeably monstrous. I motioned for Mara to feel free to go, and she snatched her handbag and stomped out without even a look toward Allison.

Allison's eyes went wide and she appeared as though a child with her hand trapped in the treat container. "What amount of that do you think she heard?"

"What the heck do you think, Allison?" I asked mockingly, getting up and assisting her with excursion of her seat.

"Where are we going?" She asked, resting every last bit of her weight on me, so I needed to almost drag her out and to my mother's vehicle, which I was getting while I was visiting the area.

"I'm taking you to your folks' home," I replied, driving her into the rearward sitting arrangement and closing the entryway.

35

In the wake of calling Mara and discovering that she had returned a taxi to her folks' home. I got into the passenger seat of the vehicle and pulled away from the café.

Chapter 6:

"I'm not whipped," I demanded, frowning at a giggling Will as we sat in a bar the night prior to his wedding.

"You're the meaning of whipped," Will remedied. "Sabrina could berate you to lick soil the floor, and you'd do it."

"You're overstating," I said.

He surrendered in mock acquiescence. "Just somewhat. The fact of the matter is that she has you at her mercy, and you appear to be entirely happy with it."

"Is there any valid reason why he shouldn't be?" Carter inquired. "She's his beginning and end, and he ensures that she knows it. What's going on with that? Additionally, she generally shows appreciation for all that he accomplishes for her. Their relationship is two-sided, adjusted. It's invigorating."

"Uh... much obliged, Carter," I said, thankful for the reinforcement, however a little stressed over the way that I was unable to let know if he was lauding my relationship or censuring his own. "Is it accurate to say that you are alright? Are things with you and Allison great?"

He moaned. "Truly, not actually. She's been constraining me to propose to her for as far back as month. That is to say, I love her, yet I simply don't believe we're prepared."

Will sneered. "What difference would it make? You two have been together for similarly as long as me and Mara."

Carter unexpectedly snapped. "That is by and large what she said, and I'm tired of it. She is continually contrasting us with you and Mara. 'Will and Mara have exceptional date evenings put away. Will and Mara are getting hitched. You know, Will does as such thus for Mara. Will would've done various stuff.' Why is it that she is continually contrasting me with you? I'm not you, and she isn't Mara, however some of the time, I'm almost certain that she wants to be."

"What do you mean by that?" Will asked, totally negligent of what Carter was inferring.

Carter snickered pompously. "I imply that she doesn't check out me the way that Mara takes a gander at you or the way that Sabrina takes a gander at Dru or even how she takes a gander at you, the manner in which she's checked out you since secondary school. At the point when I check out Allison, I don't feel needed. I feel like I'm being utilized as something to have your spot, yet for reasons unknown, I just can't do it right."

An abnormal quietness wrapped the table for the following couple of moments as we as a whole paused for a minute to handle what was recently said. Will looked confounded. Carter looked amazed that he'd let the entirety of that slip, and I was simply attempting to figure out how to diffuse the circumstance.

"How about you simply part ways with her, Carter?" I proposed.

He looked down in disgrace. "I may need to. I can't continue to do this."

Will picked then to express up his feeling. "I believe you're by and large excessively touchy. Allison is stunning. She merits somebody who isn't simply going to abandon her."

"Definitely, perhaps that was your involvement in her, Will," Carter jeered, "however you've destroyed her for any other individual. She wants somebody that will be your clone, and I'm not that person. That's all there is to it."

What's more with that, Carter stood and beat a hurried retreat out of the bar.

Will shook his head in dismay. "For what reason is everybody unexpectedly tracking down an issue with Allison?"

"You must be joking," I murmured, running my hands over my face.

"What? What am I missing? I must be missing something. You've never loved her. Carter is abruptly saying that she's not over me, and Mara believes she's been acting off of late."

"Stand by, you intend to let me know that your life partner is worried about Allison's conduct, you actually fail to really understand what's happening?"

He shrugged. "I thought she was simply blowing up."

"You didn't tell her that, did you?"

"That is to say, better believe it. Why? Would it be advisable for me to not have?"

In spite of how unfunny the circumstance was, I was unable to do everything except chuckle a bit. "God, I have a simpleton for a closest companion."

"Would could it be that I'm missing, Dru?" He argued.

"Everybody is correct, Will," I informed him. "Allison isn't over you. She never moved past you."

He almost fell over in giggling. "Better believe it, right. I know Allison. I'd know whether that was valid."

Shaking my head, I said, "You know, I'd regularly concur with you, yet this whole circumstance has shown me how unmindful you truly are, Will. Open up your eyes and look the hellfire around, man. You're the one in particular that doesn't see it."

He unexpectedly looked shaken as mine and every other person's words at last soaked in. "Indeed, what am I expected to do about it?"

"Be straightforward with me, Will. In case Allison wouldn't have parted ways with you, do you believe that you two could in any case be together?"

"No doubt, I do."

"Do you at any point wish that you were with Allison rather than Mara?"

"I wouldn't agree wish, however I'd lie in case I said that I don't ponder what my future with Allison would resemble each time I see her, that I don't contrast Mara with her occasionally."

"Would you discard yours and Mara's whole relationship assuming Allison conceded to in any case being enamored with you?"

He began to say no, however he faltered, truly contemplating his reply, and I realized that I wasn't going to like it.

"I don't have the foggiest idea," he conceded.

I gestured gravely, feeling terrible for Mara. "Then, at that point, it sounds to me like you shouldn't get hitched."

He unexpectedly got protective, frowning at me. "Why should you address me on marriage? You've been with similar individual for a very long time and still haven't proposed. It looks to me like you're not close to as quite a bit of a specialist as you're attempting to give off an impression of being at present."

Regardless of his forceful tone, I remained quiet. "This isn't about me and Sabrina, Will. This is about the way that you're wedding Mara tomorrow when there's plausible that you could in any case be infatuated with Allison. I'm not occupied with let individuals know how to direct their connections. I was simply giving you my viewpoint as your closest companion. You want to sort your crap out, Will, and quick."

That was all I said prior to taking cues from Carter and departing the bar.

Chapter 7:

After dropping Allison off at her parents' house and checking up on Mara, I headed back to my parents' house. It was about one in the morning, so I quietly made my way through the front door and out the back one into the fenced-in backyard where Carter and I always used to come to think when we were growing up. From the looks of it, I wasn't the only one who had some thinking to do. Carter was sitting on his side of the bench that was in the center of the picturesque garden-like yard.

"Hey," I greeted, approaching him and taking my place on my side of the bench.

"Hey, Bri," he replied, sounding like he'd been through it.

"Wanna talk about it?" I asked.

"Do you?" He countered, probably reading my demeanor like I read his.

I nodded, and we spent the next twenty minutes recounting the terror that was our night to each other.

"Why didn't you tell me about all of this stuff with Allison earlier, Carter?" I asked.

"I didn't want to see the look of pity on your face," he admitted, "the one you're giving me right now.

I sighed, shaking my head. "I'm not pitying you, Carter. I'm upset because you're my brother, and I didn't know that you were suffering like this. You deserve better. Break up with her."

My brother put his head in his hands, the same way I do when I get anxious. "Dammit, this is not why I decided to talk to you about this."

"Then, why did you decide to talk to me about it?"

"I was hoping that you'd talk me out of breaking up with her, tell me that we should work through it.

"I don't think you should. I don't think it's fair that you're putting in so much effort to constantly get written off by her. Plus, Capricorn and Libra are absolutely terrible together, so this relationship was doomed from the start," I explained.

"Thanks, Bri," he said sarcastically. "You really know how to make a guy feel better about his deteriorating relationship."

"I all seriousness, Carter, do what your heart tells you to, but if you're not sure, clear your head and get some rest. Decide in the morning."

He nodded thoughtfully, and we both stood and started to head inside, but we were stopped by Dru suddenly coming out the back door looking upset, and I instantly knew that he needed to talk.

"Dru, what's wrong?" I inquired, curious as to what could make my easy-going, level-headed boyfriend this upset.

"I'll see you guys in the morning," Carter announced, quickly excusing himself from the impending conversation.

"Dru..."

"This whole damn wedding is cursed," he spat, pacing frustratedly.

I walked up to him and grabbed his hands, leading him to the bench to sit, so he'd stop pacing. "What do you mean?"

"We were wrong about Will. Mara should be worried. She doesn't deserve this."

I was having a really hard time trying to string together his nonlinear thoughts. "Dru, calm down. What's going on? What were we wrong about?"

He took a deep breath before looking at me intently and telling me what he was trying to tell me. "I asked

Will if there was any chance that he'd go back to Allison if she asked him to."

I knew where this was going, but that didn't stop me from trying to give Will the benefit of the doubt. "And he said no, right? I mean there's no chance that-"

"He said that he doesn't know."

"Are you fucking kidding me?" I yelled, jumping up and starting to pace. "What the hell? What am I going to tell Mara?"

"Nothing," he replied instantly. "We're done being in the middle of other people's relationships."

"But she's my best friend. I can't just let her marry him when he's still in love with someone else."

"I get that, I do, but that kind of news isn't something that should be coming from us. Will has to figure his shit out for himself."

"At the expense of Mara's heart?"

"Hopefully, it won't come to that." Dru sighed, seeing that I was extremely upset by what he'd told me. "I'm sorry, Bri. I shouldn't have-"

"No," I snapped, stopping suddenly to look at him. "Don't do that. Don't ever apologize for not hiding something from me. Always tell me everything. No secrets, remember?"

He sighed. "Yeah."

"Now, will you make me a promise?" I asked, looking at him in the eyes as I took a seat next to him on the bench.

"Of course."

"If at any point something about us changes for you and you no longer love me as much as you used to, promise me that you'll let me know."

"Sabrina, that's never going to-"

"Promise me."

"I promise. Now, will you do something for me?" He asked.

"Anything."

He stood and held out his hands for me to take, which I did. He pulled me to my feet so that we were standing face-to-face and said, "I know that you were worried about stealing Will and Mara's thunder, but considering that this wedding is probably going to shit tomorrow, I don't think there's very much thunder to steal at this point..."

He trailed off, but I smiled, knowing exactly what he was implying. I reached around that back of my neck and undid the necklace that I kept tucked into my shirt, holding it out to reveal the stunning diamond engagement ring, hanging from it. I slid it off the chain and gave it to Dru, who happily slipped it onto my left ring finger.

"It looks much better there," he whispered, leaning his forehead against mine.

I smiled giddily, kissing him quickly. "I love you."

"And I love you," he replied.

Chapter 8:

"Have you talked to Mara yet?" I asked Will as I fixed my tie.

It was a few hours before the wedding and we were getting ready at his parents' house.

"About what?" He said, taking a seat on a nearby chair.

"About Allison," I responded dubiously, glancing at him over my shoulder. "If there's any chance that you'd leave Mara for her, Mara deserves to know."

"There's nothing to talk about," Will insisted. "Ali was my first love, and there are always going to be some feelings there. If it were up to me, would the relationship have ended? No. But it did. I'm with Mara now, and I love her."

"You're sure?"

"I'm more sure of Mara than I have been of anything else in my life."

I nodded, breathing a sigh of relief. "Glad to hear it."

There was a quick knock at the door before Carter came rushing in. "Sorry, I'm late."

"No problem, man," Will replied.

"What took you so long," I inquired. Judging by his slightly stressed and frantic demeanor, it had something to do with Allison.

"Allison and I were talking," Carter answered, confirming my suspicions.

"And…" I prompted, waiting on him to elaborate.

Carter sighed tiredly. "We decided to try to work it out."

I sighed, wondering how Allison had managed to sucker him into that decision, but otherwise masked my disappointment.

"Well, that's great," Will said, eyeing me pointedly. "Right, Dru?"

"I just hope she's worth it, man," was my simple response.

~*~

Sabrina's POV

A few hours before the wedding, Mara and I were in one of the many rooms in Will's parents' house getting ready. She was sitting in front of the mirror and I was standing behind her working on her hair.

"Are you sure you don't want me to give Allison the boot? It's not too late," I insisted.

"No," Mara said. "I want her up there with us. I want her front and center when I marry the man that she claims to love. She wants to play this like a game, then it can be a game. I want her watching when I win."

I took a second to look at my best friend, put off by her out of character declaration before speaking again. "I mean, that was a little aggressive, but go off I guess."

We briefly made eye contact in the mirror before breaking down into uncontrollable, side-splitting laughter, finding everything that had just transpired way funnier than we should have. Mara's laughter suddenly halted as she squinted at something in the mirror and then smiled happily.

"I'm glad to see you finally wearing that in its rightful place," she said, catching me off guard.

I confusedly followed her gaze to my engagement ring. "What do you mean, finally? I-"

"Cut the shit, Bri. I know that you and Dru have been engaged for the past five months. I helped him pick the ring."

"Oh," I replied stupidly.

"He also told me that you were going to wait to wear it until after my wedding," she continued. "Something about not wanting to steal my thunder and cosmic karma, which is the stupidest thing I've ever heard, by the way."

"Well, I changed my mind," I told her, putting the final pin in her hair.

"Good," Mara said, standing to hug me. "You should never put yourself second for me. I would've been just as happy as I am now had you told us all when it happened."

"Yeah?"

"Of course."

Our moment was rudely interrupted by a knock at the door.

"Come in," Mara called, wiping a few stray tears off my face that I didn't even realize had fallen.

Allison strolled in, looking victorious. "Sorry I'm late," she announced, not looking very sorry at all.

"Where have you been?" Mara inquired, taking a seat on the chaise, as I took up residence in front of the mirror to start on my makeup.

"I had to talk Carter out of breaking up with me," she started to explain. "He said he was tired of putting in a bunch of effort just to be written off by me.

You know, that doesn't really sound like Carter. I wonder where he got it from," she said, staring me down.

"I'm surprised you know what Carter sounds like at all. It tends to get hard to hear over the constant sound of your voice," I shot back, never looking away from my reflection in the mirror.

Allison almost growled as she approached where I was sitting. "Look, I know you had something to do with his sudden burst of confidence. Just understand this. You need to stay the hell out of my relationship, Sabrina."

Finally losing my composure, I slammed down the makeup brush in my hand and whirled to face Allison. "No, you understand this. If you are not truly in love with Carter, then let him go. This is your only warning because if you hurt my brother, Allison, I will ruin you."

She scoffed. "Ruin me?"

"You're a beauty blogger, Allison, on with a substantial fanbase. It took you years to build up your following. It's a shame how easy it would be to tear it all down."

The room was silent as the weight of my threat sunk in. After a few minutes, I pulled Mara up off the chaise. "Let's get you dressed!"

Chapter 9:

Well, we'd finally made it. It was time for Mara and Will to say their I-dos. We were all standing at the altar, the priest beginning his whole spiel.

"Dearly Beloved, we are gathered here today to join Will and Mara in matrimony commended to be honorable among all. Into this-these two persons present now come to be joined. If any person can show just cause why they may not be joined together-let them speak now or forever hold their peace."

All of our gazes subtly drifted to Allison, who wasn't paying any attention. She seemed to be deep in thought. When the moment passed and she said nothing, we all but sighed in relief, looking back at the priest.

The priest nodded before continuing. "Now, Will, repeat after me. I, Will..."

"I Will..."

"Take you, Mara..."

"Take you, Mara..."

"To be my wife..."

"To be my-"

"Stop!" Allison suddenly shouted, causing a collective gasp to go through the crowd.

Mara shot me and S.O.S. look, and I nodded, grabbing Allison's arm and lowering my voice. "What the hell do you think you're doing?"

"I'm going after what's mine," she replied.

"He's not yours anymore, Allison. You screwed that up, remember?"

She snatched her arm out of my grip. "We'll see about that." Before I could catch her again, she had stepped in between Mara and Will.

"Allison!" I called.

"Will, please don't do this," Allison begged. "Don't marry her. If you still feel anything for me, you won't do this."

"Ali..." Will whispered, looking at her with something like longing.

Mara quickly shoved Allison out of the way to face her fiance. "Will, tell her there's nothing there." Instead of reassuring Mara, Will stayed silent, causing Allison to smile victoriously. "There's nothing there, right?"

Will shook his head defeatedly. "Mara, I-I don't know."

"Wow..." Mara breathed, taking a step back.

"But I love you more, Mara," Will insisted. "I love you more than anything. I want to marry you."

He reached out to take Mara's hand, but she snatched it away, retreating back towards me. "No, that's bullshit. This wedding is bullshit. Our entire relationship has been bullshit! I'm done." With that, she turned to me, holding back the tears so she wouldn't cry in front of all of her family and friends. "Get me out of here."

I nodded, wrapping an arm around her shoulders and quickly leading her away from the ceremony.

Chapter 10:

Back in Mara's dressing room, I was trying my best to calm her down as she cried hysterically.

"What am I supposed to do now, Bri?"

"Well, you can't marry him after that," I said, kneeling in front of her and dabbing at her face with a tissue.

"I know," she insisted. "At least, my mind knows, but I still want to. Is that weird? Despite everything that just happened and everything I just said, I still want to be with him. I still want to marry him."

"And I'm not saying that you can't one day. I just don't think that you guys are ready to do it now, Mar. You have a lot of stuff to work through. Marriage isn't something that should be rushed."

With one last little sniffle, Mara nodded and said, "You're right."

"Alright. You clean yourself up, and I'm going to tell everyone that the wedding is off," I announced, standing. "At least they'll enjoy the reception."

"No," Mara called, stopping me from leaving the room. "I should do it. Just give me a second."

I nodded and waited by the door as she took a few more minutes to compose herself, and touch up her makeup. When she finished, we linked arms and headed back out to face the anxiously waiting crowd.

When we got back out there, we found all the guests whispering amongst themselves, Dru looking like he was talking Carter down from something, Allison pacing, deep in thought, the priest still in his spot, seeming rather confused, and Will sitting on the edge of the altar, staring down at the ground. I let Mara go as she went to stand in the middle of the altar, catching everyone's attention.

"Hi, guys," she started, with a small smile. "I...um...I just have a few things to say. First, Will, I love you, and I do want to marry you. I just don't think we're ready yet. We obviously have some issues to work out first."

We all snuck looks at Allison. Well, all of us except for Will, who was staring at Mara gratefully. She spared him a smile before returning to addressing the guests.

"However, it is my sincerest hope that this wedding does not have to go to waste. There is a couple here that has been together twice as long as me and Will. They've been secretly engaged for the past five months. They're truly right for each other. The stars couldn't have written it more perfectly, or you know, however that stupid astrology thing works. Anyway, Sabrina and Dru, it would be my honor if you would take my dream wedding. After all, it's half Sabrina's dream too."

Dru and I locked eyes from opposite sides of the altar. I stood there, frozen in place by shock. As Dru crossed over to meet me, seemingly in slow motion, a thousand thoughts crossed my mind, but I came to one conclusion. I loved Dru. I loved him with everything in me, and I had every day for the past eight years. I wanted nothing more than to marry him, so fuck everything that could possibly go wrong because I was going to marry him. Today.

"What do you say, Bri?" Dru whispered when he'd finally reached me. "You wanna get married?"

"Dru, I wou-" I started, but he cut me off.

"Look, I know this isn't what you had planned."

"Dru."

"I know that the stars are probably all wrong for this."

"Dru."

"I know that you are probably going through everything that could possibly go wrong, but-"

"Dru, shut up! Yes."

"Yes?" He said, confusedly.

I chuckled a little at his surprised demeanor. "Yes, let's get married."

Before we could say anything else, Mara turned to ask, "So?"

Dru smiled broadly at me before turning his attention back to Mara. "Looks like we're getting married."

Mara squealed excitedly, grabbing me by the hand and pulling back toward the door.

"Where are we going?" I asked.

"To hope and pray that our dresses fit each other," she replied.

Chapter 11:

"Everyone, please join me in welcoming Mr. and Mrs. Dru Conde!" I heard Mara announce as Dru and I stepped into the gorgeous garden where the wedding reception was being held.

The guests all clapped and cheered as we made our rounds. When we finally got to our table, I stopped and took in just how much the seating had changed from the engagement party a month and a half ago. Dru and I were now seated in the middle. Carter was seated to my left and Mara was next to him across from me, Will was sitting in between Dru and Mara, and of course, we were sans Allison.

"You know," Mara started, "I'm still trying to figure out how my wedding dress looks better on you than it does on me."

I shrugged dramatically. "I guess the stars were aligned perfectly."

"Is that really how it works?"

"No," I replied, laughing a little, "but it's nice to think so, isn't it? Do you have my purse?"

"Mm-hm."

She handed me my clutch and I removed a cell phone from it, and before I could do anything with it, Dru snatched it out of my hands.

"Your work phone, Bri? Really?" He asked dubiously.

"Things still need to go on as I planned. Somebody has to do it," I defended, reaching for the phone which he moved further away from me.

"Then get someone to do it, but not you, not today."

"I'll do it," Mara exclaimed, reaching for the phone which Dru gratefully relinquished to her. "How do you do it?" She asked with just as much enthusiasm as before, but now, a look of confusion was on her face as she stared down at all the contacts on the phone.

"One tab has the schedule, another has all the contacts you need," I explained.

She nodded confidently. "Okay, seems easy enough."

"Thank you, Mara," Dru said, giving her a small, gracious smile.

"No problem," she responded nonchalantly. "Now, everybody squeeze in. We need a group selfie."

"Really, Mar?" Carter whined playfully.

"Shut up and get in the picture, Carter."

We all crowded in for the picture. As Mara snapped the photo, something caught my attention in the background. It seemed Allison had seen us and was now beating a hasty retreat. Judging by the way my brother stiffened next to me, he'd noticed her too.

"Go," I whispered to him.

"What?" He replied, playing dumb.

I rolled my eyes. "I know you have something to say to her after that stunt she just pulled. Go say it."

"Bri, I-"

"You know," I said, cutting off whatever excuse he was about to give me, "in the dressing room today, Allison told me that you'd grown a backbone and stood up to her. Where is it now?"

"I'm just not confrontational outside of the courtroom, Sabrina. You know that."

"The courtroom can't be the only place you assert yourself, Carter," I insisted exasperatedly. "If it is, you're going to get run over by people like Allison your whole life."

He nodded. "You know what? You're right."

"I usually am," I muttered, causing him to give me a withering look.

"I'll be right back."

With that, Carter stood and made his way over to Allison, who had seen him coming and stopped by the exit. I watched as she tried to muster up an apologetic smile.

"Hey," Allison greeted, quietly.

"We need to talk," I said, not falling for the fake apologetic front she was putting up.

"I figured as much," she said, looking like she was going to cry, but I knew better. "Carter, I'm sorry. I shouldn't have done that. It was a momentary lapse in judgment. I-"

I cut her off. "Stop it, Allison. Are you really still trying to defend yourself after that? There's no coming back from that shit. *We* can't come back from that."

"Yes, we can," she insisted. "I know I screwed up, but I love you. Sure, we have some issues to work through, but-"

"No. *You* have *a lot* of issues to work through, but you'll be doing it without me. I'm done with trying to work through this."

"What are you saying?"

"I'm done with you, Allison. I suggest you stay here and move in with your parents. I'll have your things shipped to you when I get home."

"You can't kick me out, Carter."

"Considering that I'm paying the bills on the apartment, I think I can," I corrected.

"Carter, you can't do this," she begged. "My whole life is in Boston. My friends, my career, my-"

"Your career?" I said, laughing a little. "You're a beauty blogger. You can take a computer with you anywhere, and until you can save up the money to be on your own, I suggest that anywhere is here in Seattle," I concluded, turning to walk away.

~*~

Dru's POV

We all watched Carter try to walk away from Allison when she dug her nails into his arm. Sabrina tensed and stood, going towards Carter and Allison, her instinct to go to her brother's rescue kicking in full force. I followed closely behind, keen to watch my wife beat the shit out of Allison if it came down to it.

"Let go of me, Allison," we heard Carter demand, trying to break free of Allison's grip.

"No. Not until you hear me out," she begged angrily.

"No. I'm done hearing you out," he replied. "Now let me go before I call security."

"You wouldn't do that. Carter, you're just upset, and I understand why, but-"

"Are you fucking deaf?" Sabrina asked, snatching Allison's hand off of Carter. "He said to let him go."

"And once again, your sister comes to your rescue because you're a pathetic little boy who can't fight his own battles."

I cringed a little at that statement because if I knew my wife like I thought I did, Allison had just sealed her fate and it was not a pretty one.

"Leave," Carter demanded before Sabrina had a chance to retaliate. He had honestly probably just saved Allison's life.

"Excuse me," Allison asked, disbelievingly.

"Get out," Sabrina commanded. "He didn't stutter."

"You know, I seem to remember telling you to stay out of my relationship, Sabrina," Allison said, finally giving Bri her full attention.

"And I seem to remember telling you that if you hurt my brother, I would ruin your life," Sabrina shot back, her tone dangerously calm.

If Allison knew what was good for her, she would've backed off then and there, but alas stupidity knows no bounds.

"I'd love to see you try, bitch," Allison challenged.

Before Sabrina could reply, Allison grabbed a glass of champagne off of a passing waiter's tray and tossed it in Sabrina's face. The room went silent, and everything from then on happened so fast it was almost a blur. Without a second thought, Sabrina backhanded Allison before snatching her by the hair and slinging her to the floor. Still mindful of getting her dress dirty, Sabrina settled for relentlessly landing kicks to Allison's abdomen. All Allison could do at that point was attempt to protect her face. By this time, Mara and Will had joined Carter and me.

"Should we get Sabrina?" Carter asked.

I shook my head in amusement. "I feel like we should, but I just can't bring myself to do it."

"I'm so tempted to help her out," Mara admitted.

"I think someone already called security," Will announced. "We should really get her."

"Fine," I conceded, going to retrieve my livid wife.

I quickly but carefully approached Sabrina, placing my hands on her shoulders and gently pulling her away. "Calm down, Bri. I think you made your point."

Sabrina relaxed, backing away from Allison's cowering frame. "Somebody get her out of here," she commanded before quickly exiting the garden without another word.

Chapter 12

"Have you conversed with Mara recently?" Dru asked, coming into our work space where I was getting my soothsaying and arranging sheets free from everything to do with the wedding I'd quite recently completed yesterday.

"No. She won't get the telephone," I replied, putting the name of another couple at the highest point of my sheets. "I'm stressed over her, Dru."

Dru moved his seat from his work area to mine with the goal that he could sit close to me. "I know, however you need to give her some time. They were together for a very long time. It must be difficult to go through treatment just to understand that your relationship is broken unrecoverable."

I jeered indignantly. "It's clearly not very hard for Will. Have you conversed with him recently? Is it true that he are Allison actually shacking up together?"

"Last I checked, yet that was about a month prior."

I required a moment to ponder how much everything had changed in the beyond a half year. I was currently five months pregnant, Mara and Will's couples treatment endeavor was a complete disappointment, and presently Mara had gone off the framework while Will moved back to Seattle to be with Allison.

I shook my head. "I disdain that those two get to have a glad closure, and Mara is left behind harming. It's not reasonable."

Dru murmured, scouring my back. "I know. What about we go visit her this end of the week?"

"No doubt?" He gestured. "OK."

"Up to that point," he began, peering down at the names of the couple whose wedding I was going to begin arranging, "you have a wedding to design. You know, assuming somebody had let me know that a half year after the whole wedding trial, you'd plan Carter's wedding, I'd have chuckled in their face."

Maybe perhaps the greatest change in the beyond a half year was that my sibling had gotten connected with to his secondary school darling. Try not to misunderstand me, I was glad for him, yet everything just appeared to be somewhat abrupt to me.

"Right?" I concurred. "That is to say, I realize that it doesn't ordinarily take individuals eight years, however a half year is somewhat quick, correct? It's not simply me?

"They dated for a long time in secondary school, Bri, and would you say you weren't the person who urged them to reunite?"

"All things considered, no doubt."

"Furthermore their star graphs check?"

"Definitely."

"So what's the issue?" He inquired. "At the point when you know, you know."

"Did you know when we met?" I asked inquisitively.

"Unmistakably," he addressed promptly and unhesitatingly.

I snickered daintily, shaking my head, not exactly trusting him. It was basically impossible that he could've known way in those days.

"What?" He asked, looking somewhat annoyed that I was snickering at him.

"We were sixteen, Dru. It's basically impossible that you knew."

"Is it accurate to say that you are questioning me?"

"Indeed. In case you knew, for what reason did it take you eight years to propose?"

He shrugged casually. "I needed to be out of school, all alone, and stable for some time."

"I surmise that appears to be legit," I pondered, insightfully.

We passed into a short, insightful quiet that was broken by Dru. "Why you never chosen to design a second service for us, Bri? I realize that wasn't actually a for you amazing wedding."

He was correct, it wasn't, yet for reasons unknown, I'd never felt leaned to design a subsequent wedding. "I don't have the foggiest idea. Shockingly, the idea never entered my thoughts."

"Truly? You never got a terrible inclination about anything? The stars didn't holler at you, or you know, but it works?"

I snickered a bit, shaking my head. "Mm-mm. I'm great. We're great. We'll generally be great."

"Simply great?" He provoked.

I feigned exacerbation, yet remedied myself regardless. "Extraordinary, stunning, awesome, foreordained, written in the stars, all of the abovementioned."

He grinned. "That is better."

"Anyway you need to put it, it's you and me against the world. I love you, and that is the one thing that I needn't bother with a star graph to tell me."

www.ingramcontent.com/pod-product-compliance
Lightning Source LLC
Chambersburg PA
CBHW071950120726
48001CB00005B/2118